Nabile Fares

Exile: Women's Turn

A Poem of East and West

L'exil au féminin
poème d'Orient et d'Occident

translated with an introduction by
Peter Thompson

Diálogos
DIÁLOGOSBOOKS.COM

Exile: Women's Turn
by Nabile Farès
a translation of *L'exil au féminin*, Copyright © Editions L'Harmattan.
English translation by Peter Thompson.
Translation copyright © 2017 by Peter Thompson and Diálogos Books.

All rights reserved. No part of this work may be reproduced
in any form without the express written permission
of the copyright holders and Diálogos Books.

Front cover photo by Marc Garanger, © Marc Garanger,
from *Femmes Algeriennes 1960*. Used by permission.

Printed in the U.S.A.
First Printing
10 9 8 7 6 5 4 3 2 1   17 18 19 20 21 22

Library of Congress Control Number: 2017945520
Farès, Nabile
Exile: Women's Turn / Nabile Farès
with Peter Thompson (translator)
p. cm.

ISBN: 978-1-944884-26-0 (pbk.)

DIÁLOGOS
AN IMPRINT OF LAVENDER INK
DIÁLOGOSBOOKS.COM

Acknowledgments

The translator is indebted to Nabile and Michèle Farès, for copyright permission, and to the Roger Williams University Provost's Foundation for The Promotion of Scholarship and Teaching.

About the Front Cover

Special thanks to Marc Garanger for donating the cover photograph, included in his well-known collection, *Femmes Algériennes 1960*.

In 1960, as the Algerian war was drawing to a close and imprisoned Algerians were being released and resettled, the French government decreed that all of them should be given French-style ID cards, so that their movements could be tracked. Garanger, a French army conscriptee with experience in photography, was given the task of photographing more than a thousand women for this purpose. These women, most of whom had never had their faces uncovered outside of their homes, were stripped of their veils and forced to sit for the photos in front of an audience of soldiers. Their reactions to this treatment, and indeed to the whole brutal history of colonialism, can be read on their faces.

Acknowledgments

The translator is indebted to Nabile and Michèle Farès, for copyright permission, and to the Roger Williams University Provost's Foundation for The Promotion of Scholarship and Teaching.

About the Front Cover

Special thanks to Marc Garanger for donating the cover photograph, included in his well-known collection, *Femmes Algériennes 1960*.

In 1960, as the Algerian war was drawing to a close and imprisoned Algerians were being released and resettled, the French government decreed that all of them should be given French-style ID cards, so that their movements could be tracked. Garanger, a French army conscriptee with experience in photography, was given the task of photographing more than a thousand women for this purpose. These women, most of whom had never had their faces uncovered outside of their homes, were stripped of their veils and forced to sit for the photos in front of an audience of soldiers. Their reactions to this treatment, and indeed to the whole brutal history of colonialism, can be read on their faces.

Foreword

This most recent translation of Farès is the first one to follow his death (August, 2016). I had greatly looked forward to giving him the English version. He was a reader of English and an admirer of Bill Lavender's book designs.

I had also anticipated more conversations about the theme of the book. We had finished work on the manuscript, but its central image—perilous crossings of the Mediterranean—had surged back into the news. Within these journeys beats the brave, feminist heart of this book.

Farès had explained to me, about three years ago, that this poetry arose from a special moment in African migration and exile. Men, before the 1980s, had always been the ones to leave North Africa in search of work (mainly in France and Spain). They found dubious lodging—often in exploitive dormitories—and sent money home. That changed when women, in a considerable wave, undertook the sea crossing on their own. *Exile: Women's Turn* is that journey, and that sea change in women's destinies.

Farès, who treated traumatized immigrants in his psychiatric practice, was dedicated to feminine strength where he saw it in the contemporary world. But we also note that some of his emphasis derives from his Kabyle roots (near Collo, Algeria) and the strong feminine roles in Berber life and folklore. Farès was a researcher in the latter (starting with his doctoral thesis). The feminist emphasis also underlies, less obviously, the narrative in his *Exile and Helplessness* (novel, Editions Maspéro, 1976; translation, Diálogos Books, 2012).

When images were too obscure for my confident rendering, I found—as I always have—that Farès's view of poetic image was really an enjoyment of constant mutation. He looked at problems I presented as if he had never seen the image before, and immediately started embellishing and extending his earlier version. As much fun as this was, it left me thinking that the English was indeed an extension of his thought, and that I had considerable freedom (I didn't abuse it) in making his poetry intelligible in the new form. That said, the real value of his modest yet exuberant exploration of his own earlier text was how he enacted poetry's deepest genius: the frustrating but exhilarating inability to rest, to be one version—inert, defined, completed.

Women, Africa, even the process of exile—all these are protagonists in Farès's imagination. Algeria is an element that unites them. Referring to my earlier interview (*Crisolenguas*, 2008), I asked (2011) "Are you saying that Algeria will always be a protagonist in your work?"

"Yes, so long as Algeria and above all what Algerian men and women are living is a part of humanity, and as long as this preoccupation doesn't exclude the world's other peoples, such as they appear in *Le Miroir de Cordoue*, *L'Etat perdu* (untranslated), and *Exile: Women's Turn*. *L'Etat perdu* is a book about the rights to life and residence of so-called immigrants, and which talks about the relation between the *ideal* of rights for people, women, children, men, old people, and what these people actually live through, today, in the contexts of political crises, military, national and international crises. I think it's because these books touch on questions that are so dense and important to each one of us that little is said about them—as if a writer, like me, could have come from the ends of the world and a place that doesn't exist and wouldn't be recognized *in* his work. And above all because these are formulations that are not denunciations but warnings of much more serious troubles to come… which I probably owe, in some way, to my work as a writer and a psychoanalyst…"

Translation became a new protagonist for Farès, or at least a new agent in his process. Etymologically, translation "carries" this book somewhere, just as poetry carried the exile, and exile carried these women. And in his process, in his responses to queries (as above), Farès must have seen how his text of thirty years ago is carried forward, how he and I were creating a problematic return to it; translation was creating a distance, a separation, a new exile or an extension of exile. His generosity allowed this to be a positive transformation.

I have translated the above, as I did the epigraph I took the liberty of adding—by the great Algerian Assia Djebar, deceased a year before Farès.

Footnotes indicating the Berber words for moon,

sky, bride and the city of Tlemcen were supplied in the original by Farès. The poem titles, in Arabic, "El-Bahar" and "Reka'a" are, respectively, "the immensity of the sea" and "prayer."

This translation is dedicated to his widow, Michèle.

—Peter Thompson

The plowshare of my memory cuts, behind me, through shadow, while I flutter in broad daylight, among the women mixing with impunity in the crowd of men... They call me "exiled." The difference is of more weight: I am expelled from there in order to hear and bring back to my family some trace of freedom... I think I'm making this bond, but I'm only stumbling in a swamp that barely flickers with light.

—Assia Djebar

Contents

I. An illegal in language	17
Excursion	19
Orphic poem	30
Hejira, the first day	30
Signs, or Verses	38
Incident	41
Departures, the first day	48
Paces, the second day	50
Transit, the sixth day	53
Cities, the fourth day	54
Waves, the fifth day	56
Mists, the sixth day	58
All is opaque, the seventh day	59
Poem of El-Bahar	61
Madinat Zahara	64
Sura	65
The Hejira	68
Reka'a	70
The eighth day	71
The last day	72
II. Imperceptible night	75
Application	77
Dreams	90
And so :	100

Exile: Women's Turn

A Poem of East and West

to Marie-Claude Lambotte
this poem

I. An illegal in language

August 1984

Excursion

Just off the street, a glance, with rain sliding over it.
A voice speaking an inherent pain
where wind howls.

It has the shadow of a voice I know well.
A forehead where my fingers travel her wrinkles.
I sit down on a chair, near her, while she looks
at a day crisscrossed with flames.

She gazes.
Her lips move, a smile brightens the table
where, in turn, her fingers rest.
Game of strangers and love's transgression: my
breath short,
my skin un-leaved by a gigantic autumn
not yet left behind by life.

July 1985

So I think back to that first exile
when my body was caught in long waiting.
Over the evening's harsh rooms of days
conceived, water-tight, endless,
her tongue's rough lip rubbing
the wood burst open.

...the shores were no more.

Splinters of the boat
that your mouth kept
Despite the cold

I loved that overture
The one that hurtled us
Past all land.

...Shadows of the straggler.

We were surprised at their powers
In the course of their language...

They pressed us down
With their traitor knees

Taking more of our words
With each down payment

With no thought for them
We caught sight of their sails

And we were waiting for their hearths and homes
To light up in a single dot their uncaring lands.

Oh the softness of the air

Which dark prisons
Hold close in our limbs.

Docile and impassive
We awaited
The violence of shooting pain

With no thought (for us)
They settled (without us)

The age-old quarrel.

Territory of language
Youth hostile
To any wandering
In the hymns of silence.

Those buffeted by breath
And its whiff of refuge

Alphabetic hostage
Of a new moon's
Mask.

September 1984

Faithful friends
From insular eras

We would observe the winds
Rebel vowels

We observed.

The day lofted
A constellation pale

And infinite.

Heavy morning rain
Lasts at a lip's edge.

One moment, she was waiting for the rain to stop.
The next moment, we were nothing but frail shadows
in daylight…

September 1982

Orphic poem

1
Hejira, the first day

Such intense cold on the seas: greedy tongue-flicks (we wanted to adjust the sails, raise them) then hurl them over the vast sea where forces from their worlds had long howled; sham agreements dating from the beginning (to escape their shadows) (destroy them) (take) (them) (away) laws of custom and exchange we'd now transcended.

> Unsated silence in the sheets. Snapped by the tongues of far-off countries. Which, starting then, by dint of sailing, had made us stateless.

We observed the setting of sails
Stretched toward the Levant.

And having barely risen
We were beseeching.

We implored:
Rickety young women
girded for journey…

> Mad shadows of their gait
> On the grey smock of close nights
> Writings poured out of their rage
> They had stuck to the center's
> Slow construction. Only the attitudes of their
> Former improprieties.

A work of the wild voyage with its
Rustling of empty temples
Beyond the naming of beliefs.

> They kept beseeching
> Inevitable vowels
> The Ferryman of The World
> For the rightful gift
> Of lips that could be theirs.

October 1984

Such were the first signs of their hejira
On the stirring quays
A memory of notes and scores
Lifted away. Ancient ones.
Water on a lip moistened
By desire.
They wrapped their bodies
In acts never seen before:
Exemplary.

They said—
Title, Papers—If it be
That in me The Other
Was designated

A between-worlds suspended
In the gaze of the Intense.

October 1985

Then followed the sober signs
Stopping any deviation cold: gesture
From the Mother-Offering
At the moment of high truth

Men planted on the strand
Like old shore birds
Left alone...

Gates opened upon the laws of the infinite their thoughts
Reached into those parts of the mirrors where the names of tireless border crossers multiplied and a gold ring drawn on the brow of the deep where only these thoughts could follow our move.

Wanderings

Scant streets
Where languages
Arrived from hasty horizons
Spread without bitterness

Greenhouse streets
Where the world
Making a wide sign to aim at
Came to drink up the magnetic space
Of every idea.

Advances

Still we advanced
Fragile Light
In the annulment
Of their shade.

August 1985

2
Signs, or Verses

…
Absurd strides
Of the powers of Dawn
Active overflowing night
Where the lookout might watch
In the stifling
On the infringing stage
Of an alien voice
The plain anthology of long disillusion
The earth's double song
Or that which you bore along
Then, like a toy tossed onto dreams
—Toy of a cradled slumber—
It grants the dawn's wish where the resting place hovers
A weave of shadow, gesture of the arc
Blunt, attenuated, invisible
Seen, outside, endlessly
On the land's sweep and undulation
Which is finally grasped
Through untimely deletions
In the reckless criterion of the sands.

Prayer: That the wound of Red-Moon
Swept by waves of barley from the earth
onto the roadstead; every day you wrote
of the ochre overture the stripping of leaves
That a tongue murmured the redness
Of Red-Moon, wounded: oh speech
Of Agur*…

Thus came into being
Like that toy on the morning of dreams
The cradle. That cradle where the resting place
Hovered like a weave of shadow.
Illegal in language.

---

*   Berber term that designates the moon.

Your hand's gaze
borne along by gesture

By dint of erasures
Over the howl of the reckless land

Thus had barley swept
The Mother
Like a toy tossed onto the morning of dreams
Onto that former love and my subtle gambit
Reckless moment of the sands.

3
Incident

…This is how she revealed her position
The line falls across the scattered
Aggregate of villages
Now and then a rumor
Drifted up to us
Children
Of a multiplicity unformed
As we listened to the sound of worlds.

Our voyages of listening were in this way
Foreshadowings.

We listened in on the salt
And the joyous sea
She who could
One day become
The diagram of their darting forth.

I begged
Alone
In this dream
Where the cradle
Of the Red-Moon
Oh Agur Moon-Word
Where the tree endured

Subtle plaything
Of exclusion

Acute phoneme
Of being
Where the work of your tongue
Found its title.

August 1984

The sign named Other
Every day this ocher
Arrived as nomad
Wounded in tongue
In a slow undulation
Hollowed by the sea
Over the reckless
Cry-terrain of the sands.

The crossing of a dream
Of tongue-wound
On the very tongue of the tree.

And if the tongue
Breathes its poem
As a fullness
Of Iguenni*...

I—Open pages of moon-mouth—
On the red underside of those signs
That you were writing and writing alone
In the wandering
Multiplied by mirrors
Cradles, languages, solitudes...

Alone
Where I
Inferred
By a dream
By language...

---

* Berber term designating the sky.

Agur...

Iguenni...

Incidental language
The old Berber
All met in the rough bark
Of nights like My Self of words
Prisoner of the Solar
In the shape of sky or moon

    For her, the voyage
    The consecration
    This dwelling of the ineffable
    In the enclave of mysteries.

October 1983

Complete freedom
Of the shipping lanes.

We listened to the wind
Ally of our understandings
Rattling the live door
Where our liaisons
Came to register.

We listened to the rains
The recent cravings of our skin
That we stretched
So they might widen
The narrow threshold
In the gaze of Those
Yet to come

We listened to the men
Their men's assemblies
And sometimes
Lithe fears that we perceived
Like hares, or dreams, or lands
We trembled.

Women whose harvest was undone
The veil slipped over the wide
Alley of the day
Among the trees
And the night

Of your presences
Has begun to glow
...

From then on we would call
No more. And took
As our only clothes
Our resolutions
...

From then on our movements
Took the shape of cities.
Incidental ones...

4
Departures, the first day

...One of the women said, "The departure is what costs. After that comes the lovely slope of Tilisan*... then the deep, fertile plains... Running toward the rock sculpted by salt... Where young women support their bellies...
Sufferings of the new-born...

...Then... Beyond the exiles of the eye and its rim of kohl... Beyond the hardened amber... Out beyond ankles gripped by bracelets... Beyond wrists snugged in brass... Beyond the flapping dresses... Beyond the constant roll of sea-foam where men stand splattered and interpret the fate of abandoned ink-stones...

...Next... On the sands of the stars
There is the scroll of permissive constellations...
The ones pious sailors honor with their
Dreams and detours...

...Calligraphy of a gaudy moon
Accompanied by a throng of harps...

...Dazzling silence of the Winding Sheet...
...Our paths established precise distances...
Along the lines... Of the camps...

---

*   Berber name for Tlemcen

…The work of some stellar hesitation…
Movements then lent to voyages…
Armpit odors… That the long sweats
Of the day had spread over our
Bodies… Parched births called forth
Along the march of incessant waves…"

Leaning against the wood, rigging in her hand,
Another woman, trembling, said, "Even a storm
Cannot stop our progress…"

The cities lay far
Beyond our words…
Incidental…

October 1985

5
Paces, the second day

Thus,
We were moving forward
Defeated mourners
The slipstream of our difficult luring.
...
Words thrown forth in the lanes
Of voyages: murmuring of attentive
Cedars.
...
We passed by
Cut-outs of deadly ruses
Beyond a Lebanon undone
By the wrecked lay-out
Of urban zones...

October 1984

The work, the unfinished poem
Charred hands and spaces
Infinite scandal of the wanderer
Amid their glory their advancing
Quacida as starry Guide
Of the Isle of Tinos…

You, oh you! Brothers
Held up by that sign
Of the Kneeling Woman
You will cross over the ancient stage
Of a land perceived
Surrounded
Inscribed by Books.

Replies
Of oars seized
Risk on all sides
We slid along the shores
One isthmus after another
So alive
As we newly questioned
Each vowel

Beings of still more cycles of expiry

Their winded mounts

On the law of Types

The operative words of the reach
Of oceans

Insatiable locus of your lasting!

6
Transit, the sixth day

Storms over the old plowings.

Dreams of young women briefly glimpsed.

Gazes bound by your desire.

Absence!
Oh absence of the traversed lands!

June 1985

7
Cities, the fourth day

"Further on, the heaving city where young legs push before them ancient desires pressed into heavy flattened suitcases, lugged by hands reddened with age and dirt, everyone heedless of the scams on the docks.
Native star of a fourth day: we knew, we tireless women traveling the dawns, that the world must have come forth from a long explosion of the seas.
The insatiable haggle of barter, the uneven work of memory kept us on the quay, like incredulous old ladies so used to their homes, used to the abandoned shores, sovereign rivals, ancient lyricists of mountains beyond reach.
From slope to slope, quays to quays, custom house to custom house, we talked, constantly we exchanged the last news of the night, the words of the innkeeper.
When will you come join us to taste the last hour of exile?
When?
When will you come to take the last taste of the dream of civility?
When?
Exile gambit, above all languages: its lasting is bitter. We march on, through similar landscapes, on different exiles.

Exile in a time of words.
Of stone, stone wall, unfinished.
I recall the moan of that young woman calling out, and called to, whom I had named all through the ancient exiles my dream my city my language my young my gorgeous... ...wedded one...

Scattered words of uncertain speeches
Announcing the great swellings of the morning"

August 1985

8
Waves, the fifth day

"Exile's newlyweds.

The ring the voyage wears
Among the lands of transit
Tislit*
Thus are these women called.

Oh joys of renewed exile
No longer fear the endless nights
Of the heart and the Intangible
The truth of your departures
The very principle of peregrination."

Thus spoke the bird of worlds
Above the heaving swell
The scent of dream on its brow
Short-cut of its moment
Clear sign of its birth.
And the rocks of an incomplete prison
Sending these beings off toward other beings
Implicit source in the form of swaddling
From place to places
From wellspring to wellspring
Arm to arm

---
* Berber term for married woman

Up to the misty shores
Salt sprays Welcoming Places
Places of nourishment and forgetting
Obscure verses
Syntax ramified
And the instant of differentiation.

September 1985

9
Mists, the sixth day

A dream of writing taken up again
Steered wrong
Or resembling compass headings
Because of obscure language

Dream redreamed
Of the Dove
Frequenter of villages
And the Dove surprised
By movement fled
Out there
Beyond the rigging of the ships.

Dangerous exiles
The way they were put together
Resembled the ancient jousting
Of Chronos.

I loved those landscapes
The first sign of germination
Inscribed in the speech of seas
Keen chariot of betraying plains.

October 1985

10
All is opaque, the seventh day

Thus spoke the earth
Trace of the disclosing word
Object of desire fleeing
Over the long brows of the seas

Astonishment of stars
Graven on the exact day
Break-throughs in the roaring surge
Rise of old destinies
Worn down by winds
These gangways in the storm.

Thus were we exposed
On the deep lands
Young trustees
Of the ancient word
Ever out of kilter.

Our knees resembled
The sanded-down knees of the pilgrims
We'd seen one evening
Climbing toward the Splendor
Of Tinos.

It was in this way we discovered the sea

Unstable setting of the Far Country
Oh breeze from El Bahar.

And it made us think of the smell of skins
Brought to us by exiles
Lips frozen in complaint
In the anchorages
Oh raging and conquering feats
Of the Untamable.

November 1985

11
Poem of El-Bahar

Days laid open by irresolute history
Prancings of starry words
In the ineffable place of emerging
History cites the escape-way of the encounter
Of yesteryear
When the Angel came to chant the chorus
On the interrupted sand
Of scriptures.

Songs arrived in one place or another.

On the exploits of leather
Or sparklings
Kaaba, Mecca stone mounted
On the face of the god of worlds.

There exists in the difficult
Birth of all exchanges
Something other than the blind exile
Of the Other
Thrumming salt drawn near by the sails.

Punctuation of childhood
Neutral age of syllabic vanishings
Language wherein the spoken word settled
In the cut-backs of the seas.

Pure lasting
of the wandering star
The wind inscribed in caesura
The plain and the dream of an obstacle
Surging up from the world
Kneeling
Bruised
Antecedent.

Praise
Whose excitement
Offers exploit as reading
Of the word
Your voyage   My translation.

October 1984

    I saw the moorings
    of my homeland
Tremble
    at the shock
of the Invincible.

November 1985

12
Madinat Zahara*

A city named for the future of motherly thoughts
The astonishing spread of slavery
In the countries of opposing lands
In order to announce the Bosun
Abandoned deep in countless
Holds.

We watched them leave
Their hands wringing
Every tenderness seized
Visions ever held in our eyes.

Oh city of vegetal burgeoning
Assigned by history
As landmark for The Contemporary
Young city offered up to the bride.

---

* Also Medina Azahara—a city-palace built by Caliph Abd al-Rahman III in the 10th century, outside Córdoba, Spain

13
Sura

The Dove's necklace
Displaced on your throat

Your cold features of Fullness
Oh memory…

Speech of a woman burned up
By her feelings, by the Pending.

Oh tremulous veil of The Lover
At the belly of the Bride...

Over the emblem of disgust
We slept on…

Oh necessary solitudes
Of the abandoned land.

14
The Hejira

...
Dark mother of the young brides
I recall your voyages
Above villages stretched
Like steps set
In the ground of the Unaccustomed

City of the eighth letter
In the overture of My Hejira, the alif,
Dark mother of young brides

A chorus had anointed as bard
One who
In an act of pure licentiousness
Had crossed the wavering line
In pursuit of divinity.

A meeting with the eighth letter
In the course of My Hejira
Letter 'A' caught only at the end

Thus would I have invited you
To the country of long nights
In a constant recall of burnings speaking, spoken
like me, by the piercing

Clairvoyance of the law

And there would have been little lamps
Poised at the crossroads of signs
Where we might have read
The multiple nomenclature
Of the lands we'd passed through

Oh intended sign
Of naming's reach

The index in chalk
Where you've read
The gravity of a face
Light phrases
Of a mounted lamp
Wavering
And introductory

To the children
Of young brides…

October 1985

15
Reka'a

Childhoods…
Oh childhoods…
…permissive genuflections…
Beyond… the lasciviousness…
of fathers…

> I… Unknown…
> By… The World…
> The purgative sura…
> Left… by the
> Camel-drivers…
> As a sign of… development.

I wanted to see…
My desire… Oh
Dehiscent… and
Attached to her hip…
That woman… Passing by
… In the Maghrebi softness…

16
The eighth day

First poppy of the season
Plucked open by the eye

Your hand traced the design
Of a broken moment
The scent of coffee resting on the table cloth
And this flower soon carried high
In your mouth
The bird denounced

For we liked to take our time
As a memory came and went
Amid the salt sprays
Brought by waves

And thanks to them
We had heard news
Of our brother the poet
Still writing
Some very fine things…

July 1985

17
The last day

Through other places
Than ours : regarding which
She, the disaster.

"Then we learned she had
Taken up residence among us."

II. Imperceptible night

July 1984

1
Application

It was important to record each new
Birth.
High barriers had been drawn up
To interdict the coming of other worlds.

                    The women would say :

"Oh infinite confusion
Of the generic earth
The earth still craving
More bodies.
Neither the body, nor the lip
Nor the soul, nor the origin
Not even if stripped bare
Of any linguistic soil."

They would murmur :

Imperceptible night
Drawn forth from caesura
Oracle of a voice
Lost in the rupture
And in that infinite binding
Of a name.

                              The women would sing :

Oh chorus of the self-evident
The claw of the island
Birthplace of
This fog gesture

They would state :

Oh name
Oh land
Oh prestige of the powerful
Red glow of eyelashes over a flame

His Name launches
A quarrel of worlds
At the elemental puffs
From El-Bahar.

                                    The women would state :

By Me the equal
Of the ineffable

The unconfessed tongue's
Song

On the door
Of the unnamable
there is the sign
of an opening.

                                They gazed :

A body open
Measuring up to words.

                              The women approved :

There is no
Satisfying
The woe
Of your origins.

She said : (one of their number)

"Oh great reaches!
He used to tell me
About the wild shadow.

Taking the allure
Of a shattering
On my lips.

Like a word
Rising up."

                                        They said :

"The cities were far off
Beyond the incidence of our words…"

                                            (night)

She would say : shadowy law
            of its own
            type
            that night
            useless
            as substitute
            for our long
            vigils.

(dawn)

And their words
Inscribed
Deep tattoos
Over the strange land
Strange to her, The Unaccustomed

Raving full of life
They waited
Near the great fire
Glory offered up
To the luminous.

Sad casualness of The Instant
flame escaping the spark

So they opened up
The blinds of the tree

Together they fanned
The Peacock's tail

And accepted directions
As good sense.

2
Dreams

Once again
The breast
Where slept
Those ancient children
of drought.

In their sleep
These girls turned
To the universal city
Where there (still) dwelled
A work of a certain strangeness.

Seated
Before the welcoming glasses
They spoke
As if they had woken
Into a primordial dream of world.

Oh tear
Of exile
Springing forth

Like an enigma placed somewhere nearby

Like a game of being, either fixed or inscribed

Like a dream named with no name

By the whims of language.

They spoke of those long gray trails
That purposefully changed flowers to ashes, wakes to exiles
On piers still visible

And in the invading night
They queried the thousand moons
Suddenly sinking

The unknown seat of the winds :
Lofty pluralities aim your paths
Where voices mingle with songs of vast dreams
Pulling away

Evening

When the slow death of the exotic fish
Sinks through abysses of forgetfulness
On the earth of silences

Turned to the travels of the sea-swell

The curious beach
Bares itself

Harkened to those who stay.

The Works of the Anxious One
For long nights this
Is how they were seen

Blazing star of the Orient
Who beat down, Untroubled,
While in the morning eye
Rose the day's dream

Dream inscribed
Which their eyes, wide,
Abandoned to readings that flagged.

Because, long in flight,
From promise and dream, they had reached
The vault of invisible constellations.

Women wounded in their gazes
Which a certain blindness kept safe.

Unreckoned provisions from a Rival

They advanced along the sublime curve

Where suddenly the world

Gleamed in the light of a star
Pointed out by a face
High above their reign

They spoke of voyages
In shimmering tints
And sudden leaps beyond
Places the same again and covered once more
Where the white-haired and devout
Drew near.

They spoke—
Women carried along on the syllables of mothers—
About mysteries hidden in the Isle of Tinos.

The shining star smote the forehead
Of their pain...

A name given to this day
To exiles duly recorded
They simply sang
Of love's worthy sites.

3
And so :

The wandering, like a poem, bore the land with it
Childhoods vanquished on sandy plains.

There where worship was born
The married woman's solar laughter.

The world had already been parted out
Between the Ogre of the mines
And the Hydra of construction sites
By the Lord of Cities
Reached just in time.

Thus
These women resembled
Clandestine Vowels
Of unwanted languages.

On the near shores of the Levant
Other sails swelled the group.

The world clutched the stone in its belly.

They rose straining on their toes
Young women sick of so much waiting.

Lofting speech like a fountain of earth
Oars split the sea swell
In deep silent breaches.

"Never again! Never again!
We'll never belong to the Death-Kings
Of the Islands and the Parrots!

Never again!
Upon the great sky of all oceans!

Never again!"

And they urged their sails
Through the dazzlement of waves
Beaching on every shore.

On the traces they left
As if the effect of some word
Where language had taken place

A work wrought from summoning tones:
They called the group together
And (lately) stepped off into
The bluish flight of exiles.